Stories of Gre

Faye Huntington

Alpha Editions

This edition published in 2024

ISBN : 9789362924452

Design and Setting By
Alpha Editions
www.alphaedis.com
Email - info@alphaedis.com

As per information held with us this book is in Public Domain.
This book is a reproduction of an important historical work. Alpha Editions uses the best technology to reproduce historical work in the same manner it was first published to preserve its original nature. Any marks or number seen are left intentionally to preserve its true form.

Contents

CHAPTER I. ALEXANDER THE GREAT. ....- 1 -

CHAPTER II. ADDISON, JOSEPII. ....- 4 -

CHAPTER III. AGASSIZ, LOUIS JOHN RUDOLPH.............- 7 -

CHAPTER IV. BACON, FRANCIS. ....- 9 -

CHAPTER V. CÆSAR, CAIUS JULIUS. ....- 13 -

CHAPTER VI. DISRAELI, BENJAMIN..................................- 16 -

CHAPTER VII. EVERETT, EDWARD. ....- 18 -

CHAPTER VIII. FARRAGUT, DAVID GLASGOW. ....- 20 -

CHAPTER IX. GORDON, CHARLES GEORGE...................- 22 -

CHAPTER X. HANNIBAL...- 25 -

CHAPTER XI. IRVING, WASHINGTON. ....- 28 -

CHAPTER XII. JUDSON, ADONIRAM. ....- 30 -

CHAPTER XIII. KNOX, JOHN..- 34 -

CHAPTER XIV. LINCOLN, ABRAHAM. ....- 36 -

CHAPTER XV. MORSE, SAMUEL FINLEY BREESE. ....- 39 -

CHAPTER XVI. NEWTON, SIR ISAAC.................................- 41 -

CHAPTER XVII. OBOOKIAH, HENRY.................................- 43 -

CHAPTER XVIII. PENN, WILLIAM. ....- 46 -

CHAPTER XIX. QUINCY, JOSIAH..- 48 -

CHAPTER XX. RUSH, BENJAMIN..- 49 -

CHAPTER XXI. SAVONAROLA, GIROLAMO. ....- 51 -

CHAPTER XXII. TENNYSON, ALFRED...............................- 54 -

CHAPTER XXIII. ULFILA. ....- 56 -

CHAPTER XXIV. VINCENT, REV. JOHN H., D.D. ....- 58 -

CHAPTER XXV. WEBSTER, DANIEL. ....- 61 -

CHAPTER XXVI. XENOPHON. ....- 64 -

THE ROUND WORLD SERIES..- 65 -

CHAPTER I.
ALEXANDER THE GREAT.

Where shall we begin? With "A" of course, but there are so many great men whose names begin with A, I don't know how to select. However, I might as well go back a good way in the world's history, and say Alexander the Great. Since he was so great that they added the word to his name, perhaps he ought to head the list. Though mind, he is not my idea of a great man, after all.

Who was he, what was he, and when did he live? Three questions in one, and questions which when well answered tell a great deal.

He was the son of King Philip of Macedonia, and was born at Pella three hundred and fifty-six years before Jesus came to this earth. His father was a strong brave soldier, and his mother was a strong fierce woman, and their son is said to have been like them both. When he was thirteen years old he had one of the greatest men in the world for his teacher. This man's name was Aristotle.

Another "A," you see; but I shall have to leave you to discover his greatness for yourselves.

When Alexander was sixteen, his father left him to manage the country while he himself went to war.

When he was eighteen he won a great victory in the army. Very soon afterwards his father was killed, and Alexander with his great army fought his way into power, and made people recognize him as ruler of the Greeks.

From that time on, for years, his story might be told in one word, War. Battle after battle was fought and won; cities were destroyed; in Thebes, just one house was left standing, which belonged to a poet named Pindar. I know you are curious to hear why his house was spared, and I know that the industrious ones will try to look it up, and the lazy ones will yawn and say, "Oh, never mind; what do I care?"

Alexander's next wish was to conquer Persia. I am sure you would be interested to read the account of his triumphant march. The people were so afraid of him that they would run when they heard that his army was coming; sometimes without an attempt to defend their cities; and all that Alexander would have to do when he reached the town would be to march in and take possession.

This series of battles was closed at a place named Gordium.

Have you ever heard of the "Gordian knot?"

The story is, that at this place, Gordium, there was a car or chariot, which had been dedicated to the gods; and a certain god had said that whoever should succeed in untying the knot which fastened the pole of the car to the yoke, should rule over Asia. No one had been found who could untie it. But what did Alexander do when he found he could not untie it, but cut it in two with his sword! And the people accepted him as the man who was to rule!

War, war, war! The great Persian soldier, Darius, had such a high opinion of his own large army that he let Alexander get with his soldiers to a point where they could fight, and could not well be taken, and another great victory was the end of the story. When Darius saw his mistake, and tried to coax Alexander into being friends, by offering his daughter for the conqueror's wife, and a great deal of land in the bargain, Alexander replied that he would marry the daughter if he wanted her, whether her father was willing or not; and that all the land belonged to him.

Now comes a dreadful story of wrong. Alexander heard that a plot to take his life had been discovered by one of his men named Philotas, but that he had not told of it for two days. When asked why he did not, he said that the story came from a worthless source and was not to be believed. But Alexander did not trust him and decided that he should be killed. As if this was not enough, he had him tortured to make him tell the names of others who were suspected. It is said that Alexander stood by, and watched the writhings, and listened to the screams of this man who had fought by his side in many battles!

Yet he seemed sometimes able to trust people. Once, when he was sick, word came to him that his physician had been bribed to poison him. When his next dose of medicine was ready, Alexander laid the letter which told this story, before his friend, the physician, then drank the medicine, to show how fully he trusted him.

Before he was thirty-three years old this wonderful, sad life was ended! I do not know anything sadder than a great, bad man. I cannot help wondering how it would have been if Alexander had lived about three hundred years later, and met Jesus Christ. Yet he might have known Jesus as Abraham did, and David, and Samuel, and all that long list of great men.

The story of his last sickness is very dreadful. It seemed to have been brought on by his awful grief over the death of a friend. But he had such a strange way of grieving! All night he would spend in drinking liquor, and all day he lay and slept off its effects. But one morning he found himself unable to rise, and he never rose again. When he was asked who should succeed him as ruler of the kingdom, he said, "the strongest." But he gave his signet ring to one of his generals named Perdiccas.

So closed this great *little* life. The greatest soldier who ever lived, as men talk about soldiers, but an utter failure in the sight of him who said: "He that ruleth his own spirit, is greater than he that taketh a city."

CHAPTER II.
ADDISON, JOSEPH.

When I was a little girl, I sat listening one day while several gentlemen who were visiting my father, talked together, and one of them told a queer story which interested me very much, and called forth bursts of laughter from the gentlemen. Then, one said, "That is almost equal to Addison's time."

Over this sentence I puzzled. The only person whom I knew by that name was an old lame man who lived at the lower end of a long straggling street, and who was not remarkable for anything but laziness. What could the gentlemen who were visiting my father know about him, and what did they mean by "Addison's time?" I hovered around my father for quite a while, looking for a chance to ask questions, but there was no break in the conversation, so I gave it up. Something recalled the matter to me during the afternoon, and I asked a boy who lived near us, and with whom I was on quite friendly terms, if old Joe Addison had a clock that was queer; explaining to him at the same time why I wanted to know. He replied that he had seen a very large and very ugly-looking watch hanging in the shoe shop by old Joe's bench, and that Joe called it his turnip, and could take the outside casing all off, just as one could take a thing out of a box. This then was the explanation, I thought, but though we talked it over very thoroughly, we failed to see any connection between the story that the gentlemen had laughed over, and old Joe Addison's watch.

Something else came up to interest us, and we forgot all about it. And it was more than a year afterwards that I learned that my father's friends did not refer to old Joe at all, but to another Joseph Addison who was quite a different character.

I want you all to become acquainted with the real Joseph Addison; enough to know what it means when you hear him mentioned.

So, if you please, set down his name in your alphabetical dictionary: Joseph Addison.

He was born on a May-day, so it will not be hard to remember so much of his birthday. But how shall we remember the date? Well, you know the first figure of course, for as we count time, it is always one. Now jump to six. Sixteen hundred? Yes; that's it. Two more figures. What is the next figure to six? Set it down. And the next figure to one? Set that down. Now what have you? Sixteen hundred and seventy-two. A little thinking will fix that date so you will not be likely to forget it, and it is really quite nice to know just when people lived. Now what was Addison, that people are remembering him for two hundred years? First a scholar. Then he must have studied hard. Also he was an author—a poet. When he was about twenty-one he wrote a poem addressed to Dryden. Just remember that man's name, will you? Some day we will make his acquaintance. Then he translated Latin poetry, and wrote several descriptive poems. People do not seem to have thought any of them remarkable, and for my part I don't know how he made his living.

JOSEPH ADDISON.

We next hear of him as a traveller. His friends managed to get a pension for him from the king, which was to give him a chance to travel and qualify himself to serve his Majesty.

Imagine our government giving a young man a salary to travel around with, just so that he might get ready to work for it! Joseph went to France, and to Italy, and to Switzerland. Wait, did I tell you where he was born? In Wiltshire, England. His father was a minister. I don't think the government was so very good to him, though, for it forgot to pay his salary, after the first year, and he had to pay his own travelling expenses. He seems to have worked hard at his writing, and some of the poems which people read and admire to-day were written during these journeys. One named the "Letter From Italy." Some people think it is the very best of all his poems.

When he was thirty-eight years old his life began to grow brighter. His friends succeeded in getting him a government office, and there was a certain great duke about whose victories Addison made a poem for which he was paid a large price. From that time he steadily rose in power. He became secretary to Lord Halifax, and then entered Parliament. In this place he knew one thing which great men do not always learn. That was, how to keep still. He was spoken of as "the silent member." A good deal of his writing is in the form of plays which were acted in the theatres.

He had a friend named Richard Steele, with whom we must sometime get acquainted. This Mr. Steele was editor of a paper called *The Tattler*, for which Addison wrote a great deal. The paper which followed *The Tattler* was named *The Spectator*, and in these two papers are gathered some of the finest writings of the two men. Newspapers were not so plenty then as now, and *The Spectator* became famous. Everybody took it. Addison's essays which were written for it are still read and admired.

When he was about forty-six years old, he quarrelled with his old friend Steele, and they took to writing against each other in the papers, and calling one another names, like naughty children. At least Steele did; I am not sure that Addison ever stooped so low. He did not live long after that. In fact, he died in the June after he was forty-seven. He was buried in Westminster Abbey in the Poets' Corner.

Now you have been introduced to him, I hope as you grow older you will be interested to study his character.

CHAPTER III.
AGASSIZ, LOUIS JOHN RUDOLPH.

Isn't that a pretty name? When he was a little Swiss boy roaming about his home, I wonder if his mother called him Louis or Rudolph, or plain John? How many years ago was that? Oh, not so very many. It was one May day, in 1807, that he opened his eyes on this world. I don't know very much about his boyhood that can be told here. He was always a good scholar. Everybody who has anything to say of him seems to be sure of that. And on questioning them, I find they mean by it that he worked hard at his lessons and learned them. No boy or girl must think that good scholars are born so. Every one of them has to work for their wisdom. Our boy studied at home. His father was a minister. When he was old enough he was sent away to the best schools within reach, where he studied medicine. He became a famous man, but not as a physician. The fact is he was an ichthyologist. Ah, now I've caught you! Who knows the meaning of that word? Boys, are there any ichthyologists among your friends? I asked a little girl what the word meant. She did not know and turned to her tall brother who was studying Latin. "Humph!" he said. "Of course I know. It is one who understands ichthyology."

"But what is ichthyology?" she persisted.

"Why, it is—it is ichthyology, of course," he said; and that is as much as he seemed to know about it.

Really, I think we can do better than that. An ichthyologist is one who understands all about fishes. Think of the little slippery, scaly things having such a long word as that belonging to them! Where did they get it? Oh, go back to the Greek language, and ask your father, or your brother, or somebody, to tell you the Greek word for fish, and you will be able to guess the rest out for yourselves.

Well, Louis John Rudolph, when he was quite a boy, was chosen by some scientific men to study out the story of some fishes that were brought from the Amazon River. You see he must have had a good name as a student, or this honor would never have come to him. It seems he did his work well, and became so interested that he went on studying fishes. When he was about twenty-one, he began to write papers about their curious and wonderful varieties, which showed so much knowledge that scholars began to get very much interested in the student, as well as in his fishes. As the years went by, and the boy became a man and was called Mr. Agassiz, he became known all over the world for his knowledge in this direction; he grew more and more interested. He found fishes everywhere. Fossil fishes next began to interest him. What are they? Why, fishes turned to stone. He found them among the rocks of Switzerland. Very little was known about them. Agassiz undertook to find out all he could. I have not time, nor room, to tell you the story of his long hard years of work. I can only tell you that he succeeded. His name is great, because he has been a great helper to students. It is great for another reason. The more he studied the wonderful works of God, the more he seemed to learn to love and trust God. The more he read of the rocks, and the bones, scattered over the earth, the more sure he was that the Bible was true. He came to our own country when he was not much over thirty years old, and lived there for the rest of his life; always studying, and teaching others. He became a professor in Cambridge University, where he helped to build a monument for himself in the Museum of Natural History which has helped and is helping so many students. He was not an old man when he died—only about sixty-six years; but he did more work in those years than most men accomplish who live to be eighty.

CHAPTER IV.
BACON, FRANCIS.

When I was a girl in school, the teacher used to give out topics once a month for essays. One evening she gave to Fanny Rhodes this topic—"Bacon." Poor Fannie hated essays worse than any of the others, I believe, and over this subject she fairly groaned. "As if I *could*!" she said. But she did. In just a month from the day the subjects were given out, the essays were to be read. Fanny was among the first to be called forward. I ought to tell you that these monthly essays were not passed in for correction until after they were read. They were to be given to the school exactly as they came from the author's hand. So Fannie began:

BACON.

The subject assigned to me for this month is bacon. I do not see how it is possible for any one to say much on such a subject. Everybody knows all that there is to say about it. It is simply the flesh of hogs, salted, or pickled, or dried.

Before she had reached the close of this sentence, the pupils were in such roars of laughter that her voice was drowned. She looked around upon us with such astonished eyes that the thing grew all the funnier, and the boys fairly shouted.

Even the gentle teacher was laughing.

"O Fannie, Fannie!" she said at last. "Did you really think I meant *pork*?"

"Why, what else could you mean?" said bewildered Fannie. And then we all laughed again.

"Why, Fannie," said Miss Henderson, "I thought of course you would understand that I meant Lord Bacon."

"Lord Bacon!" repeated poor Fannie in dismay; "I never heard of him."

So lest you too make the same mistake, I want to introduce you, not to a piece of pork, but to Francis Bacon, who was born in London considerably more than three hundred years ago. Isn't that a long time to be remembered?

What about him? Why, he was a very learned man. A lawyer who wrote books that the lawyers of to-day study carefully.

Also he wrote essays on a great variety of subjects—essays that scholars in these days read and enjoy. In fact, as I look them over, I see many sentences which girls and boys might enjoy before they are old enough or wise enough to be called scholars. Isn't that a queer idea, that you must be quite wise before people will say of you "he, or she, is a scholar?"

I have been reading Lord Bacon's essay on "Cunning," and it certainly shows that the people who lived hundreds of years ago, were at least as cunning as they are now.

Listen to this: "It is a point of cunning, when you have anything to obtain of present despatch, to amuse the party with whom you deal, with some other discourse, that he may not be too much awake to make objections.

"I knew a secretary who never came to Queen Elizabeth of England, with bills to sign, but he would always first put her in some discourse of state, that she might the less mind the bills."

And this: "The breaking off in the midst of that, one was about to say, as if he took himself up, breeds a greater appetite in him, with whom you confer, to know more."

Did you never hear girls talk together according to this hint?

"Girls, it was the queerest thing you ever heard of! And then Minnie said—but dear me! I don't suppose I ought to tell you that—"

At which the girls are almost sure to say, "Oh, yes, do! We'll never repeat it in the world!"

It is my opinion that a great many boys and girls must have studied Bacon very carefully.

Here is another wise saying: "In things that a man would not be seen in himself, it is a point of cunning to borrow the name of the world: beginning, 'the world says,' or, 'there is a speech abroad.'"

If Lord Bacon were living in these days, he would know that the way to do it would be to commence all such sentences with "Why, they say," etc. Have you never wondered who "they" were, who are all the time saying such important, and often such disagreeable things?

FRANCIS BACON.

Lord Bacon says, "I knew one that when he wrote a letter, he would put that which was most material in the postscript; as if it had been a by matter." I have received just such letters as that, and sometimes they are from boys and girls. Remember, the great Lord Bacon does not say that it is a wise thing to do, but "a point of cunning."

I do not find that he wrote about getting into debt, but perhaps he did, for he certainly knew a great deal about it. He has the name of having been all his life in debt to some of his friends. So, wise man as he was, like most other men, we can, as soon as we begin to study his life, find something to avoid, as well as something to copy.

Yet we are to remember him as a wonderful man. Here is what one writer says of him: "A man so rare in knowledge, of so many several kinds, endued with the facility and felicity of expressing it in so elegant, significant, abundant and yet so choice a way of words, of metaphors, of allusions, perhaps the world has not seen since it was a world." That sentence was written long ago, yet men think much the same of him still.

He was not only a lawyer, but a philosopher. Now just what does that word mean? Do you know? I thought not. Let us go to the dictionary and see. "Philosopher: one devoted to philosophy." Very well, Webster, but what is philosophy? Look again. "Philosophy: the love of, or search after wisdom." Why, that is extraordinary! Then we may all be philosophers! But Webster says a great deal more about the word. If you have a bit of the philosopher in your nature, I think after reading this article, you will go at once to the dictionary, and have more wisdom after you have carefully studied the word Philosophy than you had before. Here is one more definition of the word, to give you a hint of what Lord Bacon filled his time with. Philosophy: "The science of things divine and human, and the causes in which they are contained."

I wonder if you now feel introduced to this great man? Enough so, certainly, not to think of him as a piece of pork! It is more than two hundred and fifty years since he died. He was not an old man, only about sixty-five, I believe; yet he had done a great deal of work, and will be remembered, I suppose, as long as there are books to read.

CHAPTER V.
CÆSAR, CAIUS JULIUS.

Our Alphabet would not be complete if we left out one of the most remarkable men that ever lived. Perhaps we shall discover why he is called a remarkable man.

Let your thoughts go back along the years to the first years you can remember anything about, to the times of which your father and mother or perhaps your grandfather and grandmother have told you. Farther than that. Go back in the pages of history even farther than the history of the years when our Saviour was on earth. That is a long time to think back, is it not? But our record tells us that Cæsar was born one hundred years before Christ. He must have been a diligent student, for he became learned in philosophy and science, and thoroughly understood all the arts of war. Those of you who have progressed so far in your Latin studies, are familiar with his history of the wars he waged with the Helvetii, a nation which occupied what is now Switzerland, and with a king called Ariovistus. This was a German king who had crossed over the line into Gaul, and if you have read the story of these wars, you know something of his peculiarity as a historian, as well as something of his skill in carrying on war. For seven years he waged war in Gaul, in the meantime invading Britain. After this the Senate at Rome commanded Cæsar to disband his army and return to Rome. This he refused to do except under certain conditions which were refused; and the Senate further declared that unless his army was disbanded by a certain day Cæsar would be considered a public enemy. When he heard of this decree he called his soldiers together, and by his eloquence made them feel that both he and they had been treated badly, and then he determined to go on. It was not lawful for a general to lead an army into the province of Rome unless upon occasions of coming in great triumph.

JULIUS CÆSAR.

Now I presume you have heard it said, when a person has gone too far in some undertaking to retreat, that he "has crossed the Rubicon." The Rubicon was a small stream which formed the boundary between Gaul, where Cæsar had been all this time with his army, and the Roman province. After he had made up his mind what to do, he led his soldiers across this little river. It was not much to do, but it was the important step which decided his future course.

I cannot tell you all that followed; how the leaders at Rome were terrified at the approach of the famous general, and fled pursued by Cæsar, who soon was made dictator of Rome. A little while after, hearing of a chance for a conquest in Asia Minor, he set out for Tarsus and presently sent back that famous message "*Veni, vidi, vici!*"—"I came, I saw, I conquered!"

He came back to Rome after some further triumphs in Africa, and ruled fifteen years. Though he gained his position of power unlawfully, he ruled wisely and appears to have sought to promote the welfare of his State. He made many good laws and carried forward many schemes for the general good. Among his undertakings was the revision of the calendar, in which he was assisted by some wise men who suggested the introduction of leap-years to make up for the six hours which were running behind every year.

But he had many enemies, and these conspired to take his life. When he was fifty-six years old he was assassinated in the Senate chamber. Among those who conspired against him was Marcus Brutus, who had been his friend, and when Cæsar saw the hand of Brutus uplifted against him he exclaimed, "*Et tu Brute!*"—"Thou too Brutus!" and fell down dead.

It has always seemed to me that there is a whole world of sadness in those three little words "Thou too Brutus!" There is love and reproach and despair. When a chosen friend turns against us we feel that we are undone.

Well, what have we found out about Cæsar's greatness? He was great in generalship, great in statesmanship, and great in oratory, and Macaulay says, "He possessed learning, taste, wit, eloquence, the sentiments and manners of an accomplished gentleman." What was lacking to make him truly great?

CHAPTER VI.
DISRAELI, BENJAMIN.

December 21, 1805, there came into the home of a Jewish family in London a little boy baby. They gave this little boy a long name, but it is a good name, and you will at once, upon hearing it, recall one of the most interesting stories of the Old Testament. Perhaps you have already guessed the name—Benjamin. The father was Isaac Disraeli, a wealthy Jew, and the author of several valuable books. The young Benjamin grew up and began to write, publishing his first work when he was twenty-one years old. And this first book is considered a work of remarkable merit.

He soon became interested in politics and was a candidate for Parliament when he was about twenty-seven years old. But he was defeated not only the first time but again and again. But not discouraged, he continued to work towards the point which he desired to gain, and in 1837 he took his seat in the House of Commons. He continued to hold his seat in that legislative body until his death, when he was not attending to the duties of higher offices.

He was called to very high positions; indeed to the highest honors that England has to offer her subjects. He was Chancellor of the Exchequer, which is an office corresponding to the Secretary of the Treasury in the United States. He was also prime minister in the Queen's Cabinet.

He was a man of great industry, and in addition to his public labors he wrote several novels which rank high as specimens of literary excellence. However, as a statesman and an orator he will be longest remembered. And right here I want to tell the boys an incident of his career which interests me, showing his determination and persistence in overcoming his own defects.

The first speech he made after becoming a member of Parliament was a very poor one. It is said that his manner as well as his words were so pompous and pretentious and his gestures so absurdly ridiculous that the House was convulsed with laughter. In the midst of his speech he closed abruptly and took his seat, saying with the ring of resolve:

"I shall sit down now and you may laugh, but the time will come when you will listen to me!"

And that time did come! He delivered some famous speeches in the House of Commons, and as a debater he led his party.

Boys, we build oftentimes upon our failures! We need not be discouraged if we are not successful at first. Many of our great men have made wretched work of their first efforts in the line of their ambition. But rising above their despondency, setting themselves at work anew with increased energy, they have conquered. So may you! Disraeli was admitted to the peerage in 1876, and was known as Lord Beaconsfield. Afterwards, because of some great service rendered to his country while he was a member of the Congress of Berlin, the Queen made him a Knight of the Garter. This is the very highest order of knighthood in the gift of the sovereign.

Perhaps some of you boys know something about the "Reform Bill" which passed the House of Commons in 1876, and which gave to every householder the right to vote. By this law a great many thousand men, nearly all of them working men, were made voters. Disraeli was the originator, and, the most earnest advocate as well, of that bill, which, by his energy and power in debate was pushed through. Disraeli died a few years since, and perhaps no statesman or author's death has ever called forth more newspaper notices and eulogies than his.

You will find it interesting to study the life and character of this man, whom not only England and England's sovereign honored, but who received many tributes of respect from the press of our own land.

CHAPTER VII.
EVERETT, EDWARD.

We have many records of great men, born in poverty, and with limited educational advantages, rising from obscurity to eminence, by their own efforts. Such we style "self-made men," and in these sketches of great men we shall have occasion to speak of some of these, but our "E" is not such an one. Edward Everett was the son of a clergyman, and had in his youth the best of educational privileges. That these were not misimproved may be inferred from the fact that he was twice the "Franklin Medal Scholar" in the Boston public schools. He graduated from Harvard University when not quite eighteen years old. That was in 1811. You will observe that I have not gone far back in the history of the world for a subject. This man lived in the present century, indeed, it is only about twenty years since he died. Young as he was, he was made Professor of Greek Literature at Harvard, a very few years after his graduation. But he went abroad before taking the professor's chair, in order to prepare himself better for the duties of the position. However, this preparation was to serve him in other capacities. Not very long did he serve the University in that way; his countrymen had other work for him. He had delivered some brilliant lectures at Harvard, but an oration delivered during the last visit of Lafayette to this country, settled the question, if any doubt yet remained as to his eloquence; it was on that occasion pronounced matchless, and the people of Massachusetts determined that such powers ought and should be made to do service in the political world. At the call of the people he left the seclusion of college walls and entered public life as a Representative in Congress. Later he was recalled from Washington to be the Governor of his State. Afterwards he travelled again in Europe, and settled himself in an Italian villa, with the purpose of carrying out a fondly cherished scheme of writing history. But again he was called into public life; first as United States Minister to the Court of St. James; then when he again hoped to settle to private life he was prevailed upon to accept the Presidency of Harvard College, which he held for three years; then before he could set about his cherished scheme of labor he was chosen Secretary of State under President Fillmore. This was his last official service, though he was not permitted to retire into private life. For ten years he used his wonderful oratorical powers in the promotion of public good; now, it was a lecture in behalf of some benevolent enterprise, now, in commemoration of some historical event, or again, a eulogy upon some eminent personage. When the scheme was afoot of securing Mount Vernon to be held by an association for the people of the United States, Edward Everett devoted his time, his energies and his unequalled eloquence to the accomplishment of that purpose. He travelled over the length and breadth of the land, and spoke thousands of times to appreciative audiences upon the "Character of Washington," and as the results of that long and wearisome journeying, he contributed to the cause over sixty thousand dollars. But with the first peal that heralded the beginning of the war a theme yet more inspiring was given him. The shot fired at Sumpter reached his ear, and on the twenty-seventh of the same month he was ready with a speech that rang out from Chester Square with no uncertain sound. But before the bells rang out "peace" he had ceased to speak—his lips were mute in death. Less than a week before he died—in January, 1865—he spoke in Faneuil Hall on behalf of Freedom.

In Boston, where his death occurred, there were demonstrations of profound sorrow; the flag at Bunker Hill, as well as all the flags of the city, was hung at half-mast. The church where the funeral services were held was crowded and the streets near the church were thronged with those anxious to pay respect to the memory of the gifted man; "the minute guns at the Navy Yard and on the Common boomed slowly. The church bells solemnly tolled, and the roll of muffled drums and the long, pealing, melancholy wail of the wind instruments filled the air."

Why the mourning? And why do we call him a great man? His country had honored him by choosing him to fill positions of trust, he was a scholar, a brilliant writer and eloquent speaker. Perhaps any one of these things would have made him what men call great, but this which has been said of him is worth more than position, scholarship, or eloquence: "he will longest be remembered as one whose every word and gesture was untiringly and grandly employed in animating his hearers to the best and loftiest ends."

There have been other men gifted in speech, with power of swaying the minds of the multitudes who came to listen to their eloquence, of whom this could not be said. Men who when called by their countrymen to use their power for the country's good, have thought more of furthering their own selfish purposes than of a nation's honor and prosperity, have thought more of the applause of the admiring throng than of the uplifting of the human race. Shall we not then give honor to one who so cheerfully laid aside his own cherished plans, ever ready to serve the public, doing his work so well in varied capacities, and of whom it could be said that "the annals of the country must be searched in vain to find one who had done more to advance every public interest and patriotic cause?"

CHAPTER VIII.
FARRAGUT, DAVID GLASGOW.

The portrait of Admiral Farragut presents to view one of the finest faces I have ever seen; it is a face I would choose to hang upon the walls where you boys could look upon it every day of your lives. Even the pictures upon our walls are our educators; they help to make us what we are; then let us hang up the faces of the good, the noble and the true. Let us choose carefully, that only pure and ennobling influences may be thus shed into our hearts.

David Glasgow Farragut was descended from an old Spanish family, one of the conquerors of earlier times, a Don Pedro. His mother was of a good old Scotch family, and it may be that he inherited from one side that adventurous, fearless nature which carried him through so many victories, and from the other side that sturdy independence and grand faith which was so characteristic of him. When quite a boy he entered the United States Navy as a midshipman. His father was an army officer, and Admiral Farragut tells the story of his own greatest victory in life in this way. He had accompanied his father upon one occasion as cabin boy. He says:

"I had some qualities which I thought made a man of me. I could swear, drink a glass of grog, smoke, and was great at a game of cards. One day my father said to me, as we were alone in the cabin, 'David, what do you intend to be?'

"'I mean to follow the sea!'

"'Follow the sea! Yes, be a poor miserable drunken sailor before the mast, kicked and cuffed about the world, and die in some fever hospital in a foreign clime.'

"'No,' I said, 'I'll tread the quarter deck and command as you do.'

"'No, David; no boy ever trod the quarter deck with such principles as you have and such habits as you exhibit. You'll have to change your whole course of life if you become a man.'

"My father left me and went on deck. I was stung with the rebuke and the mortification—was that to be my fate, as he had pictured it? I said, 'I'll never utter another oath! I'll never drink another drop of intoxicating liquor! I'll never gamble!'"

And those vows he kept until his dying day. This was when he was ten years old, and though he lived to be a great naval commander and won many victories, I think you will agree with me that this was the greatest of all. You know that "he that ruleth his spirit is greater than he that taketh a city." And, too, without this triumph over his own spirit, do you think he would have won those other battles which have made him famous?

During the Civil War he was put in command of an expedition against New Orleans and soon compelled that city to surrender. For this service he was promoted to the rank of rear-admiral. It was two years later that, as has been said, "he tilled up the measure of his fame by the victory of Mobile Bay." In the heat of the conflict the admiral lashed himself high in the rigging of his flag ship, so that he could overlook the scene and direct the movements of his fleet. If you wish to see the brave old man in the supreme moment of his life, you must read the account of that battle. He himself said, in speaking of the moment when to hesitate was to lose all and to go forward seemed destruction, and he had prayed, "O, thou Creator of man who gave him reason, guide me now. Shall I continue on, or must I go back? A voice then thundered in my ear, 'Go on!' and I felt myself relieved from further responsibility, for I knew that God himself was leading me on to victory."

He was honored by receiving the thanks of Congress for his services and by promotion. But worn out with his severe labors in the service of his country he was soon called to the higher reward. His work was done. His last victory was the victory over death, for he died the death of the Christian; the God whose guidance he invoked in the midst of the smoke and din of battle, gave dying grace to the old hero. He was born in East Tennessee, in 1801, and died at Portsmouth, N.H., in 1870. We are told that from boyhood he was thoughtful, earnest and studious. He was one of the best linguists in the Navy, and whenever his duties took him to foreign ports he spent his spare moments in acquiring the language of the natives. His eyes were somewhat weak and the members of his family were kept busy reading to him, in those times when he was off duty. He was thoroughly versed in all matters relating to his profession. The study of the character of a man like Admiral Farragut will be a help to any boy in the formation of his own character. The grandeur and nobility of mind, the bravery and steadfastness of soul manifested in his public life are an example to the boys of the present day.

CHAPTER IX.
GORDON, CHARLES GEORGE.

Gordon, Grant, Greeley, Garfield, Gladstone—such an array of names as sound in my ears when I think of this alphabetical list of great men! We have come to a letter that is prolific in subjects, and it is hard to choose. I would like to have you study the characters of the great men whose names I have written down above and there are others—great men whose initial letter is "G"—Gough, Garrison, Garibaldi—indeed there seems to be no end to the list! At present we will speak of only one. I have headed the list with the name of Gordon, not intentionally, but it seemed to come first. Was that because he is greatest? Perhaps not. My boys, there are noble men in this list, some of them your own countrymen, who have done much for humanity.

General Charles George Gordon was an Englishman, but his fame has gone into all the earth; his example, his Christian faith and courage, is ours to emulate. He belonged to a military family and was educated for the army, entered his country's service at twenty-one, and distinguished himself in the Crimean War. Afterwards he was attached to an expedition of the French and English into China at a time when there was a rebellion in progress, and upon application of the Chinese government to the English for an officer to lead their forces in suppressing this rebellion, Lieutenant Gordon was appointed to the command, and it was at that time that he began to be called "Chinese Gordon," a name by which he has been widely known. He was successful in suppressing the revolt which is known as the Tai-ping Rebellion. The Chinese government were loud in their expressions of esteem and gratitude and would have rewarded him right royally, if he would have accepted the reward of money; as it was, they gave him "a yellow riding-jacket to be worn on his person, and a peacock's feather to be carried in his cap; also four suits of uniform proper to his rank in token of their favor and desire to do him honor."

CHARLES GEORGE GORDON.

As he refused their money, the leading officials called upon the British ambassador and desired to know what would please the man who had done so much for them and would not be rewarded. They were puzzled over the conduct of a man who seemed to be prompted by a motive other than military glory or pecuniary reward. There has been printed a letter written to his mother about this time which shows a strong regard for his parents' feelings and wishes and a desire to put down the rebellion for the good of humanity. It was several years later that he was appointed English governor of the Soudan. He was offered a large salary, but would accept only a moderate sum. This position gave him an opportunity of fighting the slave trade. He sailed up the Nile to Khartoum, and from that city he went still farther into the interior of Africa, into the midst of a people so degraded and wretched that he wrote "what a mystery, is it not, why they were created! A life of fear and misery night and day!" And it was his happiness to minister to the needs of these people.

It is said that he gave away more than half of his small salary to soften the lot of the poor creatures, and he was so kind and gentle with them and so considerate of their needs, that unused as they were to a governor who treated them with kindness, they became devoted to him, proving over again that kindness will win even a savage heart.

During the few years he remained governor of the Soudan he was earnest in his fight against the slave dealers and accomplished much, but because the Khedive from whom he received his appointment did not support his measures, he finally resigned and returned to England. It was a sad day for the Soudan when he left; I have not time to tell you how affairs in that far-off country grew worse and worse, until in January, 1884, General Gordon was sent the second time to command the Soudan. It is said his coming was welcomed by the people who remembered his former kindness and that they "fell on their knees before him and kissed his hand as he passed along the streets." Many of you have read how the brave General was at length driven into Khartoum and forced to cut off from communication with the outside world. And finally relief being delayed the city was taken by the rebels and General Gordon killed. Thus in following the path of duty he went straight to his death. He fell in the city which he had sought to defend. He died at his post.

Boys, the life and death of this man may teach valuable lessons. There is always an attraction in stories of the exploits of a brave soldier, but when you can write after that word brave the other and best adjective of all, *Christian*, we seem to have passed the highest eulogy. General Gordon was eminently religious. It is said of him that he read scarcely anything but the Bible; and that "he was simply a Christian with his whole heart, and his religion went into the minutest details of his life."

Once when waiting in loneliness and weariness on the Upper Nile, for steamers which were delayed, he wrote: "I ask God not to have anything of this world come between him and me; and not to let me fear death, or feel regret if it comes before I complete my programme. Thank God, he gives me the most comforting assurance that nothing shall disturb me or come between him and me."

Whatever may be our political opinions, whatever we may think of the work he was set to do, and in doing which he lost his life, we are sure of one thing, this man's devotion to duty was supreme and absolute. And death found him not shirking or hiding from duty and from danger, as ever fearless and bold, walking in the line of what he considered his duty. A chivalrous Christian soldier has ended his warfare, leaving behind a fragrant memory, a shining example of Christian faith. He believed in his Leader, and followed with implicit trust, seeking not for glory, yet his heroic death has covered his name with glory.

CHAPTER X.
HANNIBAL.

Now we will go back through all the years that have rolled away since Christ came to dwell upon the earth for a time. And yet further back in the history of the world we will look for our great man. Two hundred and forty-seven years before Christ, so the chronicle runs, one of the greatest generals, and one of the most interesting characters of antiquity, was born at Carthage.

And where is Carthage, does some one ask? Ah! we must ask, where *was* Carthage? your school maps of modern geography do not indicate the location of this ancient city, which was great and powerful, and situated upon the northern coast of Africa, near the site of the modern city of Tunis. In the annals of ancient history, Carthage figures largely, although no record of its early history has been discovered. The city was destroyed 146 B.C. Another Carthage was built upon the same site, which in its turn was destroyed 647 A.D.; and of this second Carthage we are told that "few vestiges of its ancient grandeur remain to indicate its site except some broken arches of a great aqueduct which was fifty miles long."

At the time when our hero was born, the first Carthage was one of the two great and powerful cities of the world. It was about that time that Rome and Carthage began a war for the possession of the beautiful and rich island of Sicily. This was the first Punic War. The Carthagenians were defeated and obliged to give up the island to the Romans.

Hamilcar, a Carthagenian general, burning with thoughts of revenge, took his young son Hannibal into the temple and made him lay his hand upon the altar and swear eternal enmity to Rome; thus the boy grew up with this one absorbing passion filling his young soul—hatred to the Romans. When his father died, he succeeded to the command of the armies, and soon engaged in what is known as the second Punic War. He led his army across Spain and crossed the Pyrenees and marched through Gaul. You see his object was to enter Italy from the North, but the Alps lifted their proud heads, seeming to be an insurmountable obstacle lying right in the path of this great army, like a long and frowning battlement. Would you not think the soldiers' hearts must have quailed as they looked up to the snow-capped peaks and realized that unless these were surmounted their expedition must fail!

Four little words tell the story—"he crossed the Alps!" But how much of iron resolution, of endurance, of suffering, of loss of life, and of perseverance lies behind that sentence! Those who know the Alps, and who also know what it means to lead an army through difficult passes, tell us that it was an undertaking of tremendous magnitude, and it would not have seemed strange if after undergoing such fatigue and hardship, the army had been defeated by the Roman forces which awaited them at the foot of the southern slope. But this was not the case. Hannibal was the victor not only in many minor engagements, but at last he obtained a complete victory at a place called Cannæ, where he destroyed the Roman army. This battle has been considered his greatest exploit in the line of fighting. The spot where this bloody battle was fought is called the field of blood, and when we know that forty thousand men were slain there, we would almost expect to see even to this day, the soil stained with blood, and surely the stain if washed out of the soil cannot be washed out of the history of those nations.

Hannibal is spoken of in history as one of the most extraordinary men that ever lived. His crossing the Alps, his generalship when opposed to disciplined and powerful forces, his sustaining himself in the enemy's country for fifteen years, with a large army without calling upon his own country for aid, his power over his forces, which were made up of different nationalities, holding them subject to his authority, and keeping down discontent and mutiny, show him to have possessed remarkable powers and great genius. In his unflinching enmity to Rome he was true to the teachings of his childhood. From his babyhood he had been taught this lesson, that he must hate this enemy of his country, and to lift Carthage to a height of power and wealth above Rome, was the aim of his life. He knew that unless Rome could be destroyed there was always danger for Carthage. They were rivals and one or the other must go down and this was why he waged such an uncompromising war against Rome.

But our hero who set out to conquer Rome was at last conquered. After many years of success in Italy, a danger threatened his own Carthage. The Romans had determined to carry the war into Africa; and Hannibal was obliged to hasten home to defend the city. He met the Roman forces under Scipio at Zama, and was defeated and forced to sue for peace. He would not have yielded, but his countrymen compelled him to accept the terms which Rome offered, humiliating though they were. After this, troubles followed him, and finally when he was about sixty-five years old the Romans having gained in power and supremacy demanded his surrender, he fled from Carthage, and at last seeing no hope of escape or relief, he killed himself by opening a little cup hidden in a ring, containing a drop of poison, which he swallowed.

While we cannot approve his course, knowing as we do, in this Christian age, that there are better things to live and labor for than the carrying out of a plan of revenge and hostility towards an enemy, we must admire many things in the character of Hannibal. His courage, his patriotism, his unflinching devotion to the cause he had sworn to live and die for and his faithfulness to what he believed to be his duty, or as he would probably have expressed it his destiny. We must pity him that when he had grown old, disappointed and discouraged, he had no other resource in his troubles but to plunge himself into an unknown world by his own act. In those days of darkness, before the light of the Gospel was shed upon the world, it was considered a brave act to take one's own life when irretrievable disaster had befallen. While learning our lessons from the admirable traits in our hero's character, be thankful that we have that light.

CHAPTER XI.
IRVING, WASHINGTON.

Among the memoirs of my childhood none are more vivid than those connected with the school which I attended up to my tenth year; the schoolhouse, the teachers, the scholars, but above all the school books are well remembered. That was a proud and happy morning somewhere about my eighth birthday when I first carried my new American Manual to school. Now you are puzzled; you have no idea what sort of a book that was. They went out of use long ago, though in this district of which I write the old books were retained longer than in many more favored sections. The American Manual was a book of selections of prose and verse for the use of reading classes, and it was through that old book, that I became familiar with the name and writings of Washington Irving. My first lesson in pathos was "The Widow's Son;" the sad story of "George Somers" impressed me strongly and helped to form a taste for that kind of reading. There was no biographical sketch of the author in those old books, and it was not till long afterwards that I learned anything about the writer of one of my favorite sketches. Washington Irving was a native of New York City. He was of Scotch descent and early orphaned; in consequence of the death of his father his education was conducted by his older brothers, himself being the youngest son of the family. It is said that he was once in the presence of General George Washington for whom he was named, and that the great man patted the little boy on the head upon that occasion. From this you will have some idea of when our author lived. He was born in 1783, and you will remember that General Washington did not die until 1799, so that it is not impossible that this story may be true. As to what that august patting may have had to do with his future career, I cannot guess, though he might thereby have been inspired with a lofty ambition.

WASHINGTON IRVING.

I am sorry to have to tell you that as a schoolboy Washington Irving was more fond of reading stories and books of travel than of the study of his lessons; indeed it is hinted that he read his favorite books slyly, during study hours. However that may be, he managed to pick up considerable knowledge of books and of the art of composition, though he did not at first choose literature as a profession, but took up the law and failing in this he undertook commercial pursuits; making a failure in this line also, he seemed driven into literature which had heretofore been only a pastime. I have spoken of a pathetic sketch which struck my childish fancy; but perhaps Irving is quite as well known through his humorous writings as any. "The History of New York by Diedrick Knickerbocker" has been called "the most original and humorous work of the age." He spent much time abroad and was honored by the friendship of even crowned heads and received many honors; among these was a gold medal bestowed by the British crown for eminence in historical composition.

Irving never married, and when a little past fifty he settled at his country home, "Sunnyside," on the Hudson, his sister and her family his companions. But for all his devotion to a country life, Irving soon after accepted the office of Minister to the Court of Spain, and left his beautiful Sunnyside to spend four years at Madrid. During these four years he wrote delightful letters to his friends at home, telling his nieces who doted on their uncle, all about the dress and manners of the Spanish ladies.

He returned home in 1846 to spend the remainder of his life in retirement, occupying himself upon his last and greatest work, *The Life of Washington*, the fifth volume of which appeared just before the author's death in 1859. We may not know the secrets of his life, but his biographers tell us that the lady whom he expected to marry died early and that he mourned her loss always and that upon his death bed his thoughts turned towards his early love. He was fond of horseback riding and kept up the habit of taking long rides until he was an old man, and one day, when he was about seventy, he was thrown from his horse, receiving severe injuries. However, he seemed to recover from the effects of this fall and lived to be seventy-six years old, failing gradually until the end came; the light went out and one of our greatest American writers had crossed over to the other side.

CHAPTER XII.
JUDSON, ADONIRAM.

IN MEMORIAM.
REV. ADONIRAM JUDSON.
BORN AUG. 9, 1788,
DIED APRIL 12, 1850.
MALDEN HIS BIRTHPLACE
THE OCEAN HIS SEPULCHRE.
CONVERTED BURMANS, AND
THE BURMAN BIBLE.
HIS MONUMENT.
HIS RECORD IS ON HIGH.

This tells the story; indeed it tells the story of all of us. We are born, we die, and the years which are counted in between the two dates, filled with the work we do, whether we do good or evil, make up our record, and stand as our monument, or if we have not built well lie as a tumbling mass of ruins.

The inscription which I have copied is cut upon a marble tablet erected in the church in the town where the Missionary Judson was born. If we had only that record our imagination would fill it out. But we are not left to fancy him growing up an earnest Christian, going out in his young manhood to a heathen land preaching and translating the Gospel and at length dying on shipboard. We have a complete record of his life and we learn that he was the son of a New England clergyman. That he was an unusually bright boy and learned to read the Bible when he was three years old! One incident of his boyhood is rather amusing. He was very fond of solving riddles and puzzles; and on one occasion when he had worked some time over a newspaper puzzle and succeeding in solving it, had copied out his answer and carried it to the post-office. But the postmaster gave the letter to the boy's father, fearing that some mischief was brewing. The father with his accustomed courtesy and sense of propriety would not break the seal, but commanded his son to open and read the letter. The father called for the newspaper containing the puzzle and studied the boy's work. But he said nothing then or ever after either of reproof or commendation, but the next day he informed Adoniram that as he was so apt at solving riddles he had purchased for him a book of puzzles, and that as soon as he had solved all it contained he should have one more difficult. The boy was delighted; what boy who delights in riddles and puzzles would not be delighted with a new book of puzzles! But imagine if you can the boy's disappointment when he discovered the book to be a school text book on arithmetic!

Well, arithmetic sometimes proves a puzzle, even to bright boys. He was always a faithful student. He graduated at Brown University with the highest honors, being the veledictorian at commencement. So exemplary was his course while in college that the college president wrote to his father a letter of congratulation upon having such an amiable and promising son.

A year after graduation young Judson entered a theological seminary. At the time when he dedicated himself to the service of God, he consecrated himself to the work of preaching the Gospel. But it was some time afterwards that he began to think about being a missionary. A printed missionary sermon preached in England was the means of turning his thoughts to the heathen. One day while walking alone in the woods meditating and lifting his heart to God in prayer for direction, the command "Go into all the world and preach the Gospel to every creature," came to him with a new power and meaning, and he then resolved to obey the command. I suppose you have all heard the story of the haystack prayer-meeting, when four young men consecrated themselves to the work of carrying the Gospel to the heathen. About the time that Mr. Judson gave himself up to the work, he was thrown into the society of these four young men and together they planned as to ways and means of carrying out their purpose.

There were many and great difficulties in the way of carrying out their scheme. You may wonder why the way should have been so difficult; there was at that time no foreign missionary society in America to send them into heathen lands. You must remember that it was seventy-five years ago that these young Christians were fired with the spirit of missions, and though it may seem strange to you, it is a fact that the Christian people of our land had not yet had their attention turned to the work of foreign missions. The command "Go into all the world," had not reached their hearts; though the words of Christ had stood in their place in the record of our Saviour's life, yet their meaning had not yet dawned upon the hearts of his followers. And I fear that even now in our own day there are many Christians who overlook the words or read them without thought of their full meaning.

It was when the desire of these students was brought before the association of Congregational churches of Massachusetts that the matter was considered by that body, and as the result the board of commissioners for foreign missions was organized. In weakness and with many misgivings this "mother of American foreign missionary societies" was organized, but it has grown to be a power in the world of missions. Afterwards Mr. Judson became a Baptist, and together with a Mr. Rice set in motion events which led to the formation of the American Baptist Missionary Union, another society in the interests of the foreign work.

At length after many trials and a long wearisome journey Mr. Judson and his wife found themselves in Burmah, which was to be the field of their labors. For nearly forty years this devoted man labored to light up that dark country with the Gospel light. Perhaps the most important work of his whole life was the translation of the Scriptures into Burmese. In his autobiographical notes are two brief records which stand for years of hard labor:

"1832, December 15, sent to press the last sheet of the New Testament in Burmese;" and, "1834, January 31, finished the translation of the Old Testament."

While the work of translation was going on, when the New Testament was about completed, Doctor Judson was at Ava, the capital of the Burman Empire; war had broken out between Burmah and England, and as a foreigner, Doctor Judson was arrested and thrown into prison. At first he was put into the death prison, but afterwards was removed to an outer prison, but was kept heavily ironed. Mrs. Judson, alarmed for the safety of the manuscript, buried it under the house.

But at length she was permitted to see her husband, and fearing that the dampness of the soil would destroy the manuscript they devised means for its preservation. Mrs. Judson made a sort of pillow, not at all luxurious, lest some one should envy him and take it away; but she sewed the manuscript up in matting, and for months Doctor Judson slept with the precious pillow under his head. At one time when the prisoners were thrust again into the inner prison, everything was taken from them and the missionary feared that he should never again see his beloved manuscript. But the pillow proved so hard that the jailer threw it back into the prison, doubtless thinking that if the prisoner could find any comfort in that, he was welcome to it. Once again the precious package was taken from him and this time thrown away. But the Providence that watches over all the interests of his children put it into the heart of a Burmese convert to pick it up as a souvenir of his beloved missionary teacher whom he supposed was about to be put to death, never dreaming that it contained anything of value; and months afterwards he restored it to Doctor Judson. And in due time it was printed and given to the Burman world as a precious legacy from one who loved them more than life.

In all the years of his missionary labor Doctor Judson visited his native land but once. He brought three children to America to be educated and himself after a short sojourn returned to his work. But his arduous labors, together with his intense sufferings during the period of imprisonment, had enfeebled his constitution, and three years after his return he died on shipboard as he was taking a short voyage in search of health, and was buried at sea.

Doctor Judson's life of consecration, his self renunciation, can but influence the hearts of all who make it a study. I have heard of a young man who was so impressed upon reading the life of this wonderful man, that he went out into a field and there alone with Christ gave himself up to the service of the Lord. The era of foreign missionary work began with the hour when the few Christian students at Williams and Andover gave themselves to the work.

A conscientious decision may revolutionize the world.

CHAPTER XIII.
KNOX, JOHN.

I want to take you back to the sixteenth century, into rugged Scotland, and into the rugged times of that period of its history. I want to introduce to you a man of whom it was said, "No grander figure can be found in the history of the Reformation in this island, than that of Knox."

John Knox was a boy when the Reformation movement began in Germany; indeed it was ten years after that when he was ordained a priest. It was twelve years later that he avowed himself a Protestant, and thus incurred the wrath of the Cardinal. He was of course obliged to withdraw from St. Andrew's, where he held the position of teacher, and seek a place of refuge. This he found with a friend named Hugh Douglass. And the old ruins of the chapel at that place are still called "Knox's Kirk." One of his beloved friends was tried and condemned to the stake for heresy. The Cardinal whose anger he had roused was killed about that time, and Knox was suspected of having a hand in it; and, having been tried, was condemned to the galleys. For about a year he suffered as a prisoner and from illness. After he was set free he went to a town on the borders of England, were he succeeded in turning the hearts of many to the views of the Reformers. Always as he had opportunity he defended the cause of the Reformation.

He was raised to a post of honor by King Edward, receiving the appointment of King's Chaplain. He was offered a bishopric, but declined that honor. At Edward's death he was again in danger. Because the new sovereign was not in sympathy with the views which he was advocating, and not thinking it wise to throw away his life, he went to the Continent; he was for a time pastor of a church in Geneva, he became a friend of Calvin and spent two or three peaceful years.

When he returned to England the Scottish clergy burned him in effigy, and he was not well received even in England. Elizabeth was now upon the throne, but this did not seem to make matters much better for Knox.

Now I cannot tell you in the little space given me about the stormy times that followed his return to Scotland. He believed that the time had come when the Reformation in Scotland must be established, and he fought bravely with tongue and pen for its success. The young and beautiful queen of Scotland tried her powers of pleasing upon the heroic man who had dared to speak plainly of the sins even of the court. "But the faces of angry men could not move him, neither could the beauty of the young queen charm him, nor her tears melt him." He continued to preach according to his convictions, and kept it up with no lessening of power until a short time before his death. But about 1570 his strength declined; but though growing weaker physically, he seemed to lose none of his intellectual and spiritual vigor. He spoke in public for the last time November 9, 1572, and died on the twenty-fourth of the same month, holding up his hand to testify of his adherence to the faith for which he had lived and preached and toiled, and in which he was now dying. I think the more you study the character of this man, the more you will admire it. If he seemed rough, remember he lived in rough times. If he was intolerant, it was an age of intolerance, and his intolerance was exercised only where he felt that the truth was assailed.

Carlyle says: "Nothing hypocritical, foolish or untrue can find harbor in this man; a pure and manly, silent tenderness of affection is in him; touches of genial humor are not wanting under his severe austerity. A most clear-cut, hardy, distinct and effective man; fearing God without any other fear. There is in Knox throughout the spirit of an old Hebrew prophet-spirit almost altogether unique among modern men."

MR. LINCOLN AND TAD.

CHAPTER XIV.
LINCOLN, ABRAHAM.

Of course; who should it be if not our Lincoln? The name is a household word in all our homes, and I doubt if I can tell you anything which you do not already know about this great man; the story of his life and his deeds are familiar to every schoolboy. His features are well known to you all, for there is scarcely a home that has not his portrait upon its walls.

In 1809 Abraham Lincoln was born in a lonely cabin on the banks of a small river or creek in Kentucky; born to poverty, hardship and obscurity, born to rise from obscurity, through poverty, hardship and toil to the highest point of an American boy's ambition. He early learned the meaning of privation and self-denial. The accounts of his early life are somewhat meagre, but he has told us himself that he had only about one year of school-life. Think of that, you boys who are going steadily forward year after year, from the primary school through all the intermediate grades up to the advanced, then to the academy, thence to college, and afterwards to law and divinity schools, think of Abraham Lincoln's school privileges and be thankful for your own. And more, show your appreciation by your improvement of your advantages.

LINCOLN'S EARLY HOME IN KENTUCKY.

Like many of our great men, Lincoln was what we style a self-made man, and yet it seems that he owed something of his making to his stepmother. His own mother died when he was a small boy, and the new mother who sometime after came into the family was very helpful to the boy, encouraging him in his love of books, and under her guidance he became a great reader, devouring every book he could lay his hands upon. Did it ever occur to you that it might be an advantage to some of us if we had fewer books? Driven back again and again to the few, we should read them more carefully and make the thoughts our own, and perhaps the stock of ideas gathered from books would even exceed that which we gain from the multitude of books we have in these days of bookmaking. Whether you read much or little, few books or many, boys, read with careful thought. Take in and digest thoroughly the thoughts presented to you.

LINCOLN'S FIRST HOUSE IN ILLINOIS.

Well, this young man had but few books, but he seems to have laid by a number of ideas which should develop in time into acts which were to startle the world and overthrow existing institutions. He worked through his early manhood and boyhood with his hands, sometimes on a farm, sometimes as a clerk in a country store. Now as a boatman, now at clearing up and fencing a farm.

It was while engaged in this last-mentioned employment that he earned the title afterwards given him in derision by his political opponents, "The rail splitter;" but I suspect that he could have answered as did the boy who in the days of prosperity was taunted with having been a bootblack, "Didn't I do it well?"

At length the way opened—or, as I think, he by his exertions forced a way to study law, and he began his practice of the profession in Springfield, Ill.

I ought to have told you, however, that before his admission to the bar he served in the Black Hawk War as captain of a company of volunteers. He soon gained distinction as a lawyer, but presently became interested in politics.

FLATBOAT.

And from that time his history is closely identified with that of his country. To tell you of the leading incidents even of his career would be to give you in a nutshell the history of the United States for that period. His noted contest with Stephen A. Douglas, his election to the presidency, his re-election, his celebrated Emancipation Proclamation, all these matters belong to the story of the stirring events of those years of our history. Then came the sad ending of this noble life; the cruel assassination of the beloved President, and the great man of the time.

Boys, you who have studied his character, can you tell me what made Abraham Lincoln great?

CHAPTER XV.
MORSE, SAMUEL FINLEY BREESE.

Long before he reached the pinnacle of his fame, Samuel Finley Breese Morse passed many quiet summer hours on the pleasant wooded borders of the ravine overlooking the peaceful Sconondoah; and even to this day if you wander through the beautiful Sconondoah wood and hunt out its sequestered nooks, you will find here and there, cut deep in the rugged bark of old forest trees, the initials S.F.B.M., carved by his hand more than half a century ago.

Professor Morse was born at Charlestown, Mass., in 1791. He was the son of a Congregational clergyman, who was the author of a series of school geographies familiar to our fathers and mothers in their schooldays. He was educated at Yale College, and, intending to become a painter, went to London to study art under Benjamin West; but becoming interested in scientific studies he was for many years president of the National Academy of Design in New York. He resided abroad three or four years. On returning home in 1832 the conversation of some gentlemen on shipboard in regard to an experiment which had recently been tried in Paris with the electro-magnet, interested him and started a train of thought which gave him the conception of the idea of the telegraph. The question arose as to the length of time required for the fluid to pass through a wire one hundred feet long. Upon hearing the answer, that it was instantaneous, the thought suggested itself to Prof. Morse that it might be carried to any distance and be the means of transmitting intelligence. Acting upon the thought, he set to work, and before the ship entered New York harbor had conceived and made drawings of the telegraph. He plodded on through weary years endeavoring to bring his invention to perfection, meeting on every hand jeers and ridicule and undergoing many painful reverses in fortune; but for his indomitable will, he would have given up his project long before he succeeded in bringing it before the public, for all thought it a wild scheme which would amount to nothing.

In 1838 he applied to Congress for aid that he might form a line of communication between Washington and Baltimore. Congress was quite disposed to regard the scheme a humbug. But there was a wire stretched from the basement of the Capitol to the ante-room of the Senate Chamber, and after watching "the madman," as Prof. Morse was called, experiment, the committee to whom the matter was referred decided that it was not a humbug, and thirty thousand dollars was appropriated, enabling him to carry out his scheme. Over these wires on the 24th of May, 1844, he sent this message from the rooms of the U.S. Supreme Court to Baltimore: "What hath God wrought!" and connected with this message is quite a pretty little story. Having waited in the gallery of the Senate Chamber till late on the last night of the session to learn the fate of his bill, while a Senator talked against time, he at length became discouraged, and confident that the measure would not be reached that night went to his lodgings and made preparations to return to New York on the morrow. The next morning, at breakfast, a card was brought to him, and upon going to the parlor he found Miss Annie Ellsworth, the daughter of the Commissioner of Patents, who said she had come to congratulate him upon the passage of his bill. In his gladness he promised Miss Ellsworth that as she had been the one to bring him the tidings, she should be the first to send a message over the wires. And it was at her dictation that the words, "What hath God wrought?" were sent.

Success was now assured; honors and riches were his, and those who had been slow to believe in the utility of his invention were now proud of their countryman and delighted to do him homage. Upon going abroad again he was received more as a prince than as a plain American citizen, kings and their subjects giving him honor. It may be believed that even in his wildest flights of fancy Professor Morse did not dream of the rapid spread of the use of his invention, or look forward to the time within a few years, when the telegraph wires would weave together the ends of the world and form a network over the entire Continent.

A few years ago, the only telegraph wire in China was one about six miles in length, stretching from Shanghai to the sea, and used to inform the merchants of the arrival of vessels at the mouth of the river. A line from Pekin to Tientsin was opened a short time since. The capital of Southern China is in communication with the metropolis of the North, and as Canton was connected by telegraph with the frontier of Tonquin at the outbreak of the late political troubles, the telegraph wires now stretch from Pekin to the most southern boundary of the Chinese Empire, and China, ever slow to adopt foreign ideas, is crossed and re-crossed by wires; we may say the thought which came to Prof. Morse upon that memorable voyage has reached out and taken in the whole world.

CHAPTER XVI.
NEWTON, SIR ISAAC.

"Every body in nature attracts every other body with a force directly as its mass and inversely as the square of its distance." This has been called "The magnificent theory of universal gravitation which was the crowning glory of Newton's life." I doubt not many of you have struggled manfully with this law as laid down in your school-books, and, having conquered it, and fixed the principle in your minds to stay, you may like to know something about the philosopher himself. In 1642, a puny, sickly baby was supposed to be moaning away its young life in Lincolnshire, England.

SIR ISAAC NEWTON.

This child's name was Isaac Newton. He belonged to a country gentleman's family. His father having died, his mother's second marriage occasioned the giving of the child into the care of his grandmother. As he grew older he gained in health and was sent to school. Having inherited a small estate, as soon as he had acquired an education which was considered sufficient to enable him to attend to the duties of one in his position, he was removed from school and entrusted with the management of his estate. However, this young Newton developed a passion for mathematical studies which led him to neglect the business connected with his estate. He busied himself in the construction of toys illustrating the principles of mechanics. These were not the clumsy work which might be expected from the hands of a schoolboy, but were finished with exceeding care and delicacy. It is said there is still in existence two at least of these toys; one is an hour-glass kept in the rooms of the Royal Society in London.

Isaac Newton's mother was a wise woman in that she did not discourage his desire for the pursuing of his studies and for investigation. She did not say, "Now, my son, you must put away these notions and attend to your business. You have a property here which it is your duty to manage and enjoy. You should find satisfaction in your position as a country squire and consider that you have no need of further study." On the contrary, this mother allowed her son to continue his studies; he was prepared for and entered the college at Cambridge when he was eighteen. From that period until his death, at eighty-five, he devoted himself unweariedly to mathematical and philosophical studies.

You all know the story of the falling apple. He had been driven by the plague in London to spend some time at his country-seat in Woolstrop, and while resting one day in his garden he saw an apple fall to the ground. Suddenly the question occurred, "Why should the apple fall to the ground? Why, when detached from the branch, did it not fly off in some other direction?"

And where do you suppose he found the answer? Read the first sentence of this article and see if *you* find it there! The truth had been the controlling power of all the falling apples since the creation, but it had never before been understood or formulated; perhaps this discovery of the law of universal gravitation gave him more renown than all his other labors put together.

He met with a sad misfortune, later, when, by the accidental upsetting of a lighted candle, the work of twenty years was destroyed. The story as told by a biographer is, that Sir Isaac left his pet dog alone in his study for a few moments, when the candle was overturned amongst the papers on the study table. It is further told as an evidence of the calmness and patience of the great man, that he only said, "Ah! Fido, you little know of the mischief you have done!"

But although he was so quiet under the great loss, the trial was almost too much for him; for a time his health seemed to give way, and his mental powers suffered from the effects of the shock. He died in 1725, and was buried in Westminster Abbey.

CHAPTER XVII.
OBOOKIAH, HENRY.

A few years ago I copied from a marble slab, imbedded in the earth upon a grave in a quiet country cemetery at Cornwall, Ct., the following inscription:

HENRY OBOOKIAH OF OWHYEE,
Died February 17, 1818, aged 26.

His arrival in this country gave rise to the Foreign Mission School of which he was a worthy member. He was once an idolator and designed for a Pagan priest; but by the grace of God, and by the prayers and instructions of pious friends, he became a Christian. He was eminent for piety and missionary zeal; was almost prepared to return to his native island to preach the Gospel when God called him. In his last moments he wept and prayed for his "Ow-hy-hee," but was submissive to the will of God and died without fear, with a heavenly smile on his face and glory in his soul.

This remarkable young man was early made an orphan by the cruel massacre of both father and mother during a fearful struggle of two parties for the control of his native island, Hawaii. His younger brother was also slain while the boy of our sketch was endeavoring to save him by carrying him upon his back in his flight. Obookiah was taken prisoner and made a member of the family of the man who had murdered his parents. After a year or two he was discovered by an uncle, and his release from the hands of his enemy secured. His uncle was a priest and he entered upon the work of preparing his young nephew for the same service. This preparation was very different from the preparation of young men in Christian lands for the work of the Gospel ministry. One part of his duty was to learn and to repeat long prayers; sometimes he was forced to spend the greater part of the night in repeating these prayers in the temple before the idols. But Henry was not happy; he had seen his parents and little brother cruelly murdered, and thoughts of the terrible scene and of his own lonely and orphaned condition preyed upon his mind continually. But he had passed through still another sad experience. Before peace was restored in the island he was again taken prisoner together with his father's sister. He succeeded in making his escape the very day which had been appointed for his death. His aunt was killed by the enemy, and this made him feel more sad and lonely than before, and he resolved to leave the island, hoping that if he should succeed in getting away from the place where everything reminded him of his loss he might find peace if not happiness; and this is how he was to be brought under Christian influences in Christian America. He sailed with Captain Britnall and landed in New York in the year 1809. He remained for some time in the family of his friend the captain, at New Haven. Here he became acquainted with several of the students in Yale College, who were at once interested in this young foreigner. From one of these friends he learned to read and write.

His appearance was not prepossessing or promising. His clothes were those of a rough sailor and his countenance dull and expressionless. But he soon showed that he was neither dull nor lacking in mental power.

For some time, while Obookiah improved in the knowledge of English, making good progress in his studies, he was unwilling to hear any talk about the true God. He was amiable and quite willing to be taught, and drank in eagerly the instruction given on other subjects, but after some months he began to pray to the true God. He had a friend, also a Hawaiian and his first prayer in the presence of another was made in company with his friend. A copy of this prayer has been preserved and I copy it for you to show how even in the beginning of his own interest in Gospel truth, his thoughts turned towards his native country.

"Great and eternal God—make heaven—make earth—make everything—have mercy on me—make me understand the Bible—make me good—great God, have mercy on Thomas—make him good—make Thomas and me go back to Hawaii—tell folks in Hawaii no more pray to stone god—make some good man go with me to Hawaii, tell folks in Hawaii about heaven"—

From this time until he died his one longing was to go back to his early home and tell the people about God. He used to talk with his friend Thomas about it and plan the work. In his diary he wrote at one time:

"We conversed about what we would do first at our return, how we should begin to teach our poor brethren about the religion of Jesus Christ. We thought we must first go to the king or else we must keep a school and educate the children and get them to have some knowledge of the Scriptures and give them some idea of God. The most thought that come into my mind was to leave all in the hand of Almighty God; as he seeth fit. The means may be easily done by us, but to make others believe, no one could do it but God only."

In April, 1817, a Foreign Mission School was opened at Cornwall. And Obookiah became a pupil in this school, intending to finish his preparation for work among his own people as soon as practicable. A description of this Sandwich Islander as given of him at that time may be of interest: "He was a little less than six feet in height, well-proportioned, erect, graceful and dignified. His countenance had lost every trace of dullness, and was in an unusual degree sprightly and intelligent. His features were strongly marked, expressive of a sound and penetrating mind; he had a piercing eye, a prominent Roman nose, and a chin considerably projected. His complexion was olive, differing equally from the blackness of the African and the redness of the Indian. His black hair was dressed after the manner of Americans."

As a scholar he was persevering and thorough. After he had gained some knowledge of English, he conceived the idea of reducing his native language to writing. As it was merely a spoken language, everything was to be done. He had succeeded in translating the Book of Genesis and made some progress in the work of making a grammar and dictionary. But the work he had planned was not to be finished by his own hand. Within a year from the time he entered the school at Cornwall he was called home. As recorded upon the marble slab, his last thoughts were for his native island; his last earthly longing was, that the Gospel might be preached to his own countrymen. One of our popular cyclopædias gives a brief mention of this remarkable young man and makes this statement: "He was the cause of the establishment of American Missions in the Sandwich Islands."

To have so lived, and by his earnestness and zeal so inspired others that upon his death they were ready to take up and carry forward the work he had planned, was to have accomplished even more than he could had he been permitted to enter upon the work for which he was preparing.

CHAPTER XVIII.
PENN, WILLIAM.

The other day I was looking at a map of Philadelphia, and at once my thoughts went back to my schooldays and the primary geography in which occurred the question, "What can you say of Philadelphia?" And the answer, "It is regularly laid out, the streets crossing each other at right angles like the lines on a checker-board." And again, "What is Philadelphia sometimes called?" Answer, "The City of Brotherly Love."

And now I wish I could set before you the calm, sweet, yet strong face of the man who founded and named this city, who truly desired it to be a city of love.

William Penn was a native of London. He was born nearly a quarter of a century after the Pilgrims landed upon Plymouth Rock; he belonged to a good family, his father being Admiral Sir William Penn of the British Navy. It appears that the son was of a religious turn of mind, and when he was a boy of twelve years he believed himself to have been specially called to a life of holiness. He was very carefully educated, but he offended his father by joining the Quakers; indeed, it seems that several times in the course of his life his father became very much displeased with him, but a reconciliation always followed, and at last the Admiral left all his estate to the son who had been such a trial to him. While a student at the University, Penn and his Quaker friends rebelled against the authority of the college and was expelled. The occasion of the rebellion was in the matter of wearing surplices and of uncovering the head in the presence of superiors. You know that the Quakers always keep their hats on, thinking it wrong to show to man the honor which they consider belongs only to God.

I cannot follow with you all the vicissitudes of Penn's life; after leaving the University he travelled upon the Continent. Afterwards he studied law in London; he became a soldier. This strikes us as being somewhat curious when we remember that the sect to which he belonged are opposed to war, and preach the doctrine of love and peace. However, he was not long in service, and meeting a noted Quaker preacher he became firmly fixed in his devotion to the society of Friends, and was ever after a strong advocate of its doctrines; nothing could turn him from the path he had chosen. He was several times imprisoned on account of his religious opinions and suffered persecution and abuse. Through all he adhered to his views, and stood by his Quaker friends in the dark days of persecution. He had inherited from his father a claim against the British Government of several thousand pounds, and in settlement of this claim he received a large tract of land in the then New World. With the title to the land he secured the privilege of founding a colony upon principles in accordance with his religious views. And in 1682 he came to America and laid the foundations not only of the City of Brotherly Love, but of the State of Pennsylvania. His object was to provide a place of refuge for the oppressed of his own sect, but all denominations were welcomed, and many Swedes as well as English people came. While other colonies suffered from the attacks of the Indians, for more than seventy years, so long as the colony was under the control of the Quakers, no Indian ever raised his hatchet against a Pennsylvania settler.

Under a great elm-tree, long known as Penn's elm, he met the Indians in council, soon after his arrival in the territory which had been ceded to him.

He said to them:

"My friends, we have met on the broad pathway of good faith. We are all one flesh and blood. Being brethren, no advantage shall be taken on either side. Between us there shall be nothing but openness and love."

And they replied, "While the rivers run and the sun shines, we will live in peace with the children of William Penn."

It has been said that this is the only treaty never sworn to and never broken.

William Penn lived to see his enterprise achieve a grand success. Philadelphia had grown to be a city of no small dimensions and no little importance. The colony had grown to be a strong, self-supporting State, capable of self-government.

"I will found a free colony for all mankind," said William Penn. Were these the words of a great man?

Unswerving integrity, undaunted courage, adherence to duty, and devotion to the service of God—are these the characteristics of a great man?

Then William Penn may well be placed in our Alphabet of Great Men.

CHAPTER XIX.
QUINCY, JOSIAH.

Counting back for five generations, we find in the Quincy family a Josiah. The great-great-grandfather of the present Josiah Quincy was a merchant, and we are told that he was a zealous patriot in Revolutionary times, and you all know that meant a great deal.

His son, who was called Josiah Junior, became a celebrated lawyer, and was prominent as an advocate of liberty. It was he who with Samuel Adams addressed the people when the British ships anchored in Boston Harbor with the cargo of tea. But notwithstanding his reputation for patriotism, his action in defending the soldiers who fired upon the mob in what is known as the Boston Massacre, brought him into unpopularity.

Yet I think that if you study the facts carefully, and weigh them well, you will see that although the presence of the British soldiers was an outrage, and justly obnoxious to the people, yet upon that occasion there was some excuse for their action. And John Adams and Josiah Quincy should not be condemned for undertaking their defence.

Afterwards both did good service in the interest of Colonial Independence. Quincy went to England doing much to promote the good of his country.

He died upon the homeward voyage in 1775, in sight of American shores. His son Josiah, three years old at the time of his father's death, was educated at Harvard University, became a lawyer, a member of Congress, and having filled acceptably various other offices, was at length elected President of Harvard, which position he held for fifteen years. He had a son Josiah, also a graduate of Harvard, and again the fifth Josiah in the line is a graduate of the same institution.

There are other Quincys of this family who have attained celebrity; among these are Edmund Quincy, who was prominent in antislavery circles.

CHAPTER XX.
RUSH, BENJAMIN.

In 1885, all over this land, we celebrated a centennial. It was not in commemoration of a victory upon the battlefield, it was not the celebration of a victory, but rather as we observe with fitting ceremonies the anniversaries of the firing of the first guns in any contest of right against wrong, so in this last centennial year we commemorated the first booming of cannon in the great war against the rum traffic, the beginning of a war that is not ended yet; all along down the century the booming has been heard, and to-day this moral fight is waging fiercely.

About one hundred and forty years before, near the city of Philadelphia, a boy named Benjamin Rush was growing up. It is said of him that as he advanced from childhood to boyhood his love of study was unusual, amounting to a passion. He graduated from Princeton College when only fifteen years old, and with high honors. He began the study of medicine in Philadelphia, but went abroad to complete his medical education and studied under the first physicians in Edinburgh, London and Paris; thus the best opportunities for gaining knowledge of his chosen profession were added to natural abilities and the spirit of research. He became a practising physician in Philadelphia, and was soon after chosen professor of chemistry in a medical college in the same city. While he is now at the distance of a century, best known as one who struck the first blow for temperance reform, yet it is interesting to know that when in 1776, he was a member of the Provincial Assembly of Pennsylvania, he was the mover of the first resolution to consider the expediency of a Declaration of Independence on the part of the American Colonies. He was made chairman of a committee appointed to consider the matter. Afterwards he was a member of the Continental Congress, and was one of the devoted band who in Independence Hall affixed their names to the immortal document which cut the colonies loose from their moorings and swung them out upon a sea of blood, to bring them at last into the harbor of freedom and independence. As was said of him at the meeting in Philadelphia, last year: "He was a great controlling force in all that pertained to the successful struggle of the colonies for national independence." We are told that "He was one of the most active, original and famous men of his times; an enthusiast, a philanthropist, a man of immense grasp in the work-day world, as well as a polished scholar, and a scientist of the most exact methods."

He was interested in educational enterprises; he wrote upon epidemic diseases, and won great honor for himself, so that the kings of other lands bestowed upon him the medals which they are wont to give to those whom they desire to honor. And now let me quote again from one who appreciates the character of this truly great man:

"This matchless physician, eminent scholar and pure patriot blent all his wise rare gifts in one tribute and cast them at the feet of his Master. He was a devout Christian."

At length his soul was stirred within him as he witnessed the increasing evils of intemperance, and he wrote and published his celebrated essay upon "The Effects of ardent Spirits upon the Human Body and Mind, with an account of the means of preventing them, and of the remedies for curing them." This is said to have been the first temperance treatise ever published—the beginning of a temperance literature. So short a time ago, just one pamphlet of less than fifty pages; now, whole libraries of bound books, besides scores upon scores of pamphlets, leaflets and many periodicals devoted exclusively to the cause of temperance! and nearly three quarters of a century after this good man had gone to his rest, men and women from all over the land thronged the city of his birth "To recount the victories won in the war—and to strike glad hands of fellowship."

And now what made Doctor Rush great? What is the best thing said of him?

CHAPTER XXI.
SAVONAROLA, GIROLAMO.

Four hundred and thirty-four years—1452-1886. What wonderful events have been taking place all along through these years since the young Girolamo first saw the light! And I have been wondering what Savonarola would have said and done had he lived in this nineteenth century. He is spoken of as one whose soul was stirred by ardent faith which burned through all obstacles; as a fervid orator and as a sagacious ruler, who evolved order out of chaos; as one who to maintain his cause of reform braved single-handed the whole power of the Papacy. He is described as a serious, quiet child, early showing signs of mental power. The books which were his favorites would, I fear, be pronounced dry by the boys of to-day. But although he was given to solid reading, he was fond of music and poetry, and even wrote verses himself. He enjoyed solitude, and loved to wander alone along the banks of the River Po. I ought to have told you that his native city was Ferrara, in Italy. He was expected to succeed his grandfather who was an eminent physician, and with that end in view he was carefully trained. But as he grew older, he found himself growing to regard the thought with disfavor, and as time went on he became convinced that "his vocation was to cure men's souls instead of men's bodies." Yet he was for a long time restrained from entering upon the priesthood by regard for the hopes and desires of his parents. But at length after having made this his daily prayer, "Lord, teach me the way my soul must walk," the path of duty became clear and he, avoiding the painful farewells, slipped away from home one day when the rest of the family were absent at a festival, writing an affectionate note of explanation and farewell. He entered a monastery at Bologna, where he gave himself up to the work of special preparation for the duties of his profession.

After some years he was sent to Florence to preach. At first his plain and severe denunciations of the prevailing sins of the time repelled the people who preferred to go where they could hear more polished and less conscience-awakening sermons, and Savonarola mourned over his apparent failure to reach the hearts of the multitude who were rushing on in the ways of sinful indulgence. But his soul was moved with zeal "for the redemption of the corrupt Florentines. He must, he would, stir them from their lethargy of sin." He was convinced that he was in the line of duty, and the more indifferent his hearers were the more anxious he grew for their awakening. Actuated by this motive he suddenly found his voice and revealed his powers as an orator. God had shown him how to reach men's hearts at last, and "he shook men's souls by his predictions and brought them around him in panting, awestruck crowds;" then at the close of his denunciations of sin, his voice would sink into tender pleading and sweetly he would speak of the infinite love and mercy of God the Father.

After a time, St. Mark's Church would not hold the crowds which came to hear him and he was invited to preach in the Cathedral. He was now acknowledged as a power in Florence, and the great Lorenzo de' Medici who was then at the height of his fame as a ruler, was alarmed, and he sent a deputation of five of the leaders of the government to advise the monk to be more moderate in his preaching, hinting that trouble might follow a disregard of this advice. But the monk was unmoved. He replied, "Tell your master that although I am an humble stranger and he the city's lord, yet I shall remain and he will depart." He also declared that he owed his election to God, and not to Lorenzo, and to God alone would he render obedience.

Lorenzo was very angry, but he tried to silence the monk by bribery, but Savonarola would not be bribed nor driven. He continued to preach with great fervor, denouncing sin in high places as well as in low. You know that in those times corruption had crept into the Church of Christ, and it was against these sins of the Church that his most scathing denunciations were hurled. He had many followers, and he pushed his reforms in Church and State. His enemies grew more bitter and fiercer. Remonstrances from those in authority had no effect. He was offered a cardinal's hat, but would not accept the conditions. He said, "I will have no hat but that of the martyr, red with mine own blood."

And this was his fate; at last he was put to death in 1498. Almost his last words were, "You cannot separate me from the Church triumphant! that is beyond thy power." In the convent of St. Mark's are preserved various relics of the martyed monk, among which are his Bible with notes by his own hand, and a portrait said to have been painted by Fra Bartolommeo. I have seen a copy of this portrait. It is in profile, with the Friar's cowl. At the first glance the expression of the prominent features seems strangely stern, but as you study the face it seems to soften and the sternness becomes sadness mingled with tenderness. One can imagine those worn and pallid features lighted up with excitement, the eyes animated and glowing with zeal, and the lips so expressive of power, relaxing into a smile even, and thus looking upon it we wonder not that crowds hung upon his words.

Hatred of sin, zeal for its removal from Church and State, seems to have been two of his strong characteristics. And he was ever bold and active in lifting up and carrying forward the standard of truth. If sometimes his zeal outran his wisdom and judgment, if sometimes his enthusiasm seemed to reach what we might call a religious frenzy in which he heard supernatural voices and saw visions, we can but believe in his sincerity and admire his boldness and commend his fearless exposure of sin. And as we study his character again and again we wonder as in the beginning of this sketch, how he would have acted in these days when sin "comes in like a flood!" Have we not need of a Savonarola? Have we not need of an army of strong, fearless men and women who shall lift up the standard of the Gospel against the tide of sin? One thought more: will each of my young readers enlist in this army and be diligent in preparing to meet the attacks of the enemy?

CHAPTER XXII.
TENNYSON, ALFRED.

The birthplace of Alfred Tennyson, Poet-Laureate, is described as an old white rectory, standing on the slope of a hill, the winding lanes shadowed by tall ashes and elms, with two brooks meeting at the bottom of the glebe field. One who has written of the poet says: "In the early beginning of this century the wind came sweeping through the garden of this old Lincolnshire rectory, and as the wind blew, a sturdy child of five years old, with shining locks, stood opening his arms upon the blast and letting himself be blown along, and as he travelled on he made his first line of poetry, and said, 'I hear a voice that's speaking in the wind;' and ever since that hour voices have been speaking to him and he has given to us the thoughts borne on winds and waves and by circumstances and surroundings, in language that we can understand. Through his poems we catch glimpses of babbling brooks, and gardens, and ivied walls; of Italian skies and summer mornings, of peaceful homes and of battle crash, and as we read we may take in the pure and grand sentiments which cannot fail to have an elevating and inspiring influence upon our hearts and lives."

Alfred Tennyson first saw the light in Lincolnshire, England, in the year 1809. His father was a clergyman, and a man of great abilities, who carefully educated his children, and from whom his sons may have inherited their poetical genius. Of their mother it has been said that "she was intensely and fervently religious, as a poet's mother should be."

The story of Alfred's first attempt at verse-making is this: one Sabbath all the elders of the family were going to church, leaving the child alone. An older brother gave him a slate and a subject, "The Flowers in the Garden," and when the family returned from service he handed the slate to his brother covered over with blank verse, then waited while the critic read! Imagine his satisfaction when the slate was handed back with, "Yes, you can write."

It is also said that the first money he earned by his pen was upon the occasion of his grandmother's death, when he wrote an elegy, at his grandfather's request, for which the old gentleman paid him ten shillings, saying, "There, that is the first money you have earned by your poetry, and, take my word for it, it will be the last."

That must have been rather discouraging. If the old grandfather could know of the honors and the money which have come to his grandson through his writings, he would doubtless be astonished.

He began to write for the press when quite young, and has written much, and I have no doubt his poems are familiar to you all. He was made Poet-Laureate in 1850.

A boy who lived in the neighborhood of Tennyson's home in the Isle of Wight, gave his definition of Poet-Laureate to a lady who asked him if he knew Mr. Tennyson.

"He makes moets for the Queen," was the boy's reply.

"What do you mean?" asked the lady.

"I don't know what they means," said the boy, "but p'licemen often seen him walking about a-making of 'em under the stars."

After Mr. Tennyson's marriage he settled at Freshwater, in the Isle of Wight. This home of the poet is described as "a charmed palace, with green walls without, and speaking walls within. There hung Dante with his solemn nose and wreath; Italy gleamed over the doorways; friends' faces lined the way, books filled the shelves, and a glow of crimson was everywhere; the great oriel drawing-room window was full of green and golden leaves, and the sound of birds and the distant sea. Beautiful in spring-time when all day the lark trills overhead, and when the lark has flown out of our hearing the thrushes begin and the air is sweet with scents from many fragrant shrubs.

"Later, when the health of Mrs. Tennyson required a more quiet place, for Freshwater had become a fashionable summer resort, the family made for themselves a new home on the summit of a high lonely hill in Surrey."

Now I might copy for you some bits out of the poems I like the best; or, I might gather here a cluster of bright gems, but I think you will enjoy the search if you each try this for yourselves instead.

Once I had occasion to select for a literary exercise "Gems from Tennyson," and I found it a delightful task, only it was hard to choose, and harder to find a stopping place. I will give the boys just one extract:

"Not once or twice in our fair island story,
The path of duty was the way to glory;
He that ever following her commands,
On with toil of heart and knees and hands,
Through the long gorge to the far light has won
His path upward and prevail'd,
Shall find the toppling crags of duty scaled
Are close upon the shining table-lands
To which our God himself is moon and sun."

CHAPTER XXIII.
ULFILA.

Long, long ago, about two centuries after our Saviour ascended into Heaven from the midst of the wondering disciples, a calamity befell a Christian family living in Cappadocia. You will find if you turn to the second chapter of Acts, that among those who listened to Peter's first sermon were men who dwelt in Cappadocia; and again Peter addresses his first epistle to the Christians in Cappadocia, or, as the revision has it, "To the elect who are sojourners" in various places, this one among others.

So you will see that the Christian religion had already, even in Peter's time, spread thus far.

Upon the occasion of an invasion of the Goths, the family of which I write was carried away into captivity. Among these pagans our hero Ulfila was born, in the year 313. His early home was upon the northern bank of the Danube. Belonging to a Christian family he was educated in the principles of the Christian religion, and became a bishop. He taught the Goths the truths of the Bible, and many embraced Christianity. Indeed, so successful were the good bishop's labors among the people, that their chief showed his displeasure by persecuting the Christians. Then Ulfila and many of his followers, those whom he had shown the way of life, left the Goths, and, securing the permission of the Roman emperor, they settled upon Roman territory.

These were afterwards called Moesogoths, from the name of the district in which they settled—Moesia. They gave up their warlike life, and became an agricultural people. And the colony increased through the immigration of others of their own people. For it seems that though Ulfila had left, the influence of his preaching did not cease, and others embraced Christianity, and as the persecutions continued these determined to join Ulfila, so it came about that through the efforts of this one man large numbers were taught the truths of the Bible. He translated the Bible into the language of the Goths. This was an immense labor, for he was obliged to invent a new alphabet.

In a public library in Upsal, Sweden, there is a curious volume known as the Codex Argenteus, or, silvered book. It is a translation of the four Gospels, and its letters are in silver, on leaves of purple vellum. This is a fragment of Ulfila's translation.

The whole work was lost for about five centuries, but was discovered, at least parts of it found, by a man named Mercator, in an old abbey of Werden, in the sixteenth century. Other parts of the New Testament have been found, but only some fragments of Ezra and Nehemiah have been discovered of the Old Testament.

We have had handed down to us very few particulars of Ulfila's life. He died at Constantinople, in 383.

CHAPTER XXIV.
VINCENT, REV. JOHN H., D.D.

I have written down the name of the "great man" which I have chosen to stand in this Alphabet, and here I pause as I reflect that to many of you his face and form and speech are familiar. You have seen him upon the platform and upon the avenues of Chautauqua and Framingham, and in other places. Some of you have welcomed him at your own homes; his smiles and his talks are among the things which will be always, so long as you live, a pleasant memory. What can I tell you about him that you do not already know? Yet I am not willing that another name should take the place of this, and therefore we will talk a little together of this friend of the young people, and idol of the older people.

Dr. Vincent's early home was in the Sunny South. "In the land of orange blossoms and magnolia groves," he first saw the light. Six years of his life were spent in the home of the flowers; then the family came North and settled in Pennsylvania.

Like the mothers of many of our great men, John H. Vincent's mother might fill a place in the book called "Some Remarkable Women."

She is described as "patient, amiable, living as though she belonged to heaven rather than earth. Often at the twilight hour, especially on Sundays, she would take her children to her own room, and there sweetly and tenderly tell them about the life to come, and point out their faults and spiritual needs."

Mrs. Bolton in her sketch of Dr. Vincent, in "How Success is Won," gives some amusing incidents of the childhood of our Great Man. I quote from memory, but I think it is she who tells the story of the boy of six years gathering the children of the neighborhood, and after getting them quiet by threatening them with the lash of a whip, he would preach to them. And so far did his zeal carry him, that upon one occasion he tore into several parts a small red-covered hymn book, which he valued as the gift of his pastor, and distributed the pieces through his audience, doubtless thinking it highly important that all should be supplied with hymn books. Whether they all sang together from the different parts of the book given them, we are not informed.

Very early in life the boy seems to have decided that he would *do something with his life worth while*; that he would do that which should help others, and realizing that there is a world to be saved, he grew up with the hope of one day becoming a minister. His studies were carried on for a time at home, afterwards at a neighboring academy. Later he engaged in teaching, continuing his studies by himself, and finally he had fitted himself for college. Not every boy would have the will and perseverance to carry on a course of study while teaching six hours or more each day. However, he did not finish his college course. Not for any want of persistence, neither did he consider such a course unimportant. But he was anxious to be about his Master's work, and thus it was that before he was twenty-one years old he set out to preach "on a thirty-mile circuit, over the mountains and through the valleys of Luzerne County, Pennsylvania."

He travelled on horseback, studying and thinking out his sermons as he journeyed. Everybody, young and old, were glad to see his bright, smiling face and feel the warm grasp of his hand. It has been said that "he never shook hands with the tips of his fingers, nor preached dry sermons."

It was during this period of his life that his mother whose parting words when he went out into the world were, "My son, live near to God; live near to God," went to be with God. One near the throne in heaven, the other living near the throne on earth; is this the secret of John H. Vincent's success in the Lord's vineyard?

REV. JOHN H. VINCENT, D.D.

At length he became a pastor, preaching for a few years in New Jersey, afterwards in the vicinity of Chicago. But all the time he was busy with plans of an educational character. These plans which were at first carried out in the establishing of Saturday afternoon classes of young people, called Palestine Classes, with the purpose of studying about the Holy Land, have at length developed a Chautauqua. I need not tell you about Chautauqua; about the C.L.S.C., nor about the C.Y.F.R.U.; you do not need to be told about the town and country clubs, nor about the society of Christian ethics. Many of you have listened to those Sunday afternoon talks in the Children's

Temple, and afterwards gone to the vesper service in the Hall of Philosophy.

I ought to tell you that although Dr. Vincent postponed his college course, he never gave it up, but outside college walls, he continued his studies by himself, even in the midst of a busy life, until by regular examinations he took his degrees, and also passed through the regular theological course of study of the Methodist Episcopal Church, to which denomination he belongs.

To the boys especially I recommend the study of the life and character of Dr. Vincent. A gentleman remarked in my hearing the other day, "probably no man living is exerting a wider influence over the hearts and minds of the young people than Dr. Vincent!" And I thought, what a responsibility! and how thankful the fathers and mothers should be that he is just the man he is; that his influence is ever on the side of truth and right; that his aim is to uplift, and that Christ is ever the centre of his thought. To see and hear Dr. Vincent is to understand something of the secret of his power. The sympathy which manifests itself in every look and tone, the enthusiasm with which he enters into his work, and which tides him over the hard places, and the personal magnetism—which makes you, whether you will or not; these qualities, sanctified and consecrated, make the man a power for good.

CHAPTER XXV.
WEBSTER, DANIEL.

A long time ago, not quite a century, however, upon a New England farm, a mischievous woodchuck was caught after much time and patience had been expended. It was the intention of the farmer's sons to put the animal to death, but the younger boy's heart was touched with pity; he begged that the captive might go free. His brother objecting, the case was carried to the father.

"Well, my boys," said the farmer, "there is the prisoner; you shall be the counsel and plead the case for and against his life and liberty, while I will be the judge."

The older boy, whose name was Ezekiel, opened the case. He urged the mischievous nature of the animal, cited the great harm already done, said that much time and strength had been spent in securing him, and now, if he were set free, he would only renew his depredations. He also urged that it would be more difficult to catch him again, for he would profit by this experience and be more cunning in the future. It was a long and practical argument, and the proud father was apparently quite affected by it. Then came the younger boy's turn. He pleaded the right, of anything which God had made, to life. He said that God furnished man with food, and all they needed; could they not spare this little creature who was not destructive, and who had as much right to his share of God's bounty as they had; could they not spare to him the little food necessary to existence? Should they in selfishness and cold-heartedness take the life which they could not restore again, and which God had given?

During this appeal tears started to the father's eyes, and while the boy was in the midst of his argument, not thinking that he had won the case, the judge started from his chair, and, dashing the tears away, exclaimed:

"Zeke! Zeke! you let that woodchuck go!"

DANIEL WEBSTER AT MARSHFIELD.

This incident I have briefly written out for you is told of the early life of the man who forty years later made his celebrated speech in the Senate Chamber in defence of the Constitution, which ended with these memorable words, "Liberty and union, now and forever, one and inseparable!"

Daniel Webster, the orator and statesman, was born at Salisbury, N.H. The house in which he first saw the light is, I think, still standing, though not as it was originally; some years ago it became the wing, or kitchen part of a new house. The farm was rugged and not very fertile; it is said that granite rocks visible in every direction, gave an air of barrenness to the scene. Among "wild bleak hills and rough pastures," his boyhood was spent. His advantages of education were limited. The family library consisted of "a copy of Watts' Hymns, a cheap pamphlet copy of Pope's Essay on Man, and the Bible, from which he learned to read, together with an occasional almanac."

He struggled with poverty through his college days, and after graduating at Dartmouth, went to Boston to study law. He is described as "raw, awkward, shabby in dress, his rough trousers ceasing a long distance above his feet." After much discouragement he was entered in a law office as a student. He was admitted to the bar in 1805, and in 1808 he married Miss Grace Fletcher. A pretty story is told of his engagement. One day he was assisting the young lady in disentangling a skein of silk; suddenly he said: "Grace, cannot you help me tie a knot that will never untie?" "I don't know, but I can try," she said.

And they tied the knot, and the writer who tells the story, says, "Though eighty years have sped by, it lies before me to-day, time-colored, it is true, but nevertheless still untied."

Mr. Webster was a member of Congress eight years; was in the United States Senate nineteen years, and a Cabinet officer five years. It is related of him that he tore up his college diploma, saying, "My industry may make me a great man, but this parchment cannot." A classmate says he was remarkable in college for three things: steady habits of life, close application to study, and the ability to mind his own business. Is it any wonder that he became a great man?

There is much in the life and character of Daniel Webster worthy of study, and many incidents are related which illustrate his greatness. One of the best things on record is this: at a dinner party given in his honor, some one asked him this question. "Mr. Webster, what was the most important thought that ever occupied your mind?" To this he replied, "The most important thought that ever occupied my mind was the thought of my individual responsibility to God."

Mr. Webster died in 1852. Thousands came to attend the funeral, and amid the sorrowing throng they laid him away in the family tomb at Marshfield. Thirty years more passed, and 1882 had come. It was then one hundred years since his birth, and again thousands upon thousands came to honor the memory of this son of New England. Men high in office—even the President of the United States—military men, scholars, judges, lawyers and ministers, men and women of the city and from the hillsides and from the valleys came to the sad, solemn celebration. And a long procession moved amid the tolling of bells, the booming of cannon, and the low, solemn dirge played by military bands.

CHAPTER XXVI.
XENOPHON.

Xenophon was an Athenian who lived about four hundred and fifty years before Christ. He was a celebrated general, historian and philosopher. He was a learner at the school of Socrates, and counted as one of his most gifted disciples. The life and the teachings of the great philosopher have been given to us by the writings of Xenophon, and his sober and practical style gives a good idea of the original. Quintilian, a Roman orator and critic, says of Xenophon, "The Graces dictated his language, and the Goddess of Persuasion dwelt upon his lips."

His style is pure and sweet, and he seems to have been a man of elegant tastes and amiable disposition, as well as extensive knowledge of the world.

Perhaps his greatest exploit as a general was the leading of the Greek troops across the mountain ranges and the plains of Asia Minor. This was after the battle of Cunaxa, where the younger Cyrus was defeated and slain. Xenophon had joined this expedition against the brother of Cyrus, Artaxerxes Mnemon, with ten thousand Greek troops. After the defeat many of the Greek leaders were treacherously murdered in the Persian camp. The Greeks were almost in despair. They were two thousand miles from home, surrounded by enemies, and the only way of retreat lay across mountain ranges, deep and rapid rivers, and broad deserts. It seemed as if fatigue and starvation and the hostility of those whom they must encounter would effectually prevent their return to their native land, but Xenophon roused them from their despondency, rallied the forces, and they began the march. It was a time of great suffering, for they had literally to fight their way. But when they reached a Grecian city after untold peril, it was found that of the ten thousand led forth, eight thousand and six hundred still remained. During the latter part of his life he lived at Corinth, having been expelled from Athens. Though the decree of banishment was revoked, he never returned. His literary work was mostly performed during these later years. Of all his writings, his Anabasis has been pronounced the most remarkable. It is a work giving an account of the nations in the interior of Asia Minor, and of the Persian Empire and its government.

He died at Corinth, in his ninetieth year.

Milton Keynes UK
Ingram Content Group UK Ltd.
UKHW040816051024
449151UK00004B/262